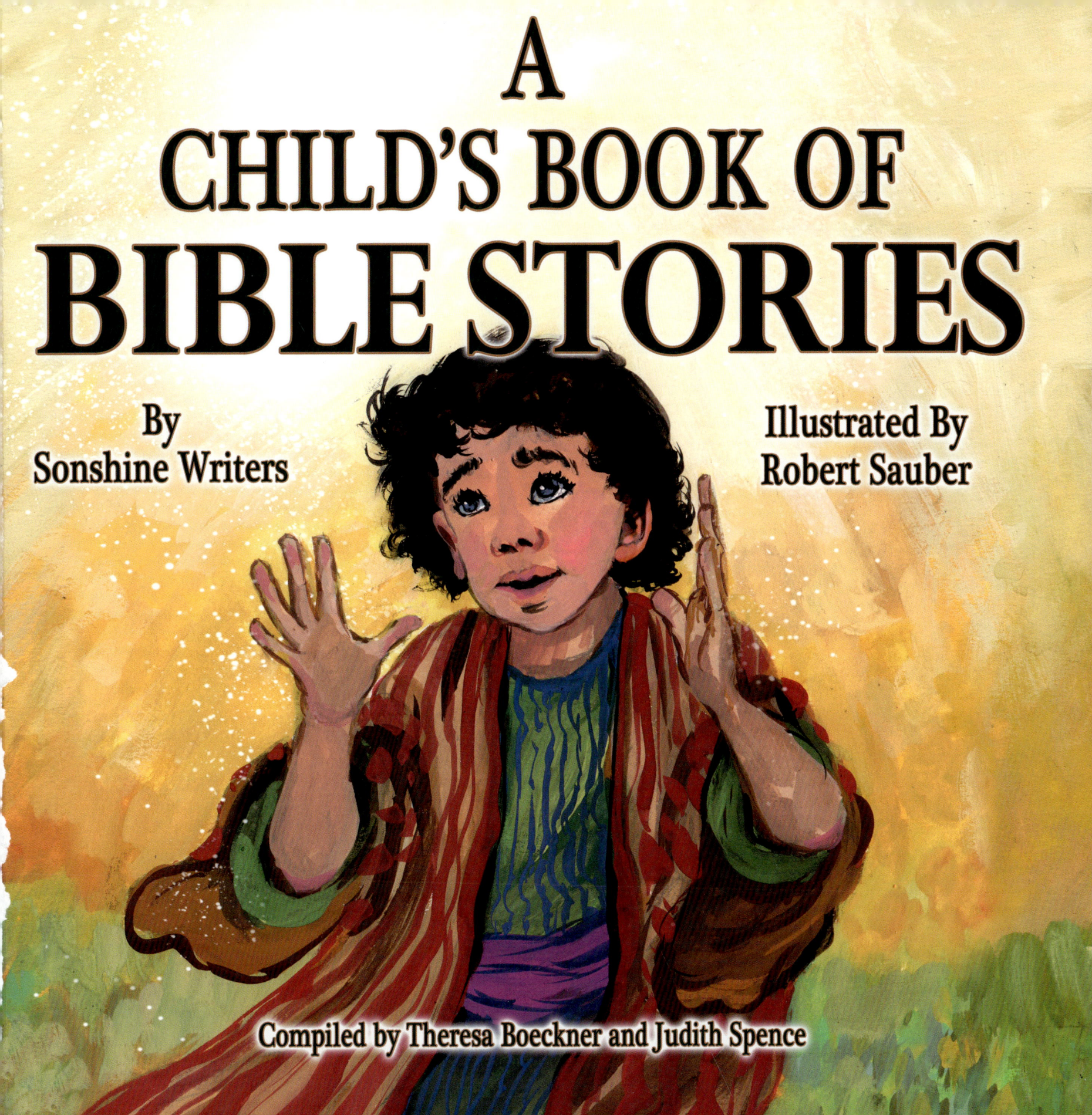

Copyright ©2019 by Theresa Boeckner and Judith Spence
Illustrations copyright ©2019 by Robert Sauber
Published in the USA
ISBN 978-7333551-0-0
All rights reserved

Because of each writer's personal writing style, some of the details in these stories will not be found in the Bible. It is not our intent to detract from Bible truths.

A CHILD'S BOOK OF BIBLE STORIES

By
Sonshine Writers

Illustrated By
Robert Sauber

Compiled by Theresa Boeckner and Judith Spence

CONTENTS

Let My People Go 1

The Widow's Oil 9

God Cares For His Friends 15

Jeremiah Speaks God's Word . . . 23

Nebuchadnezzar 31

Belshazzar 39

Jonah 47

In the Master's Vineyard 55

Welcome Home 63

Thank You, Jesus 73

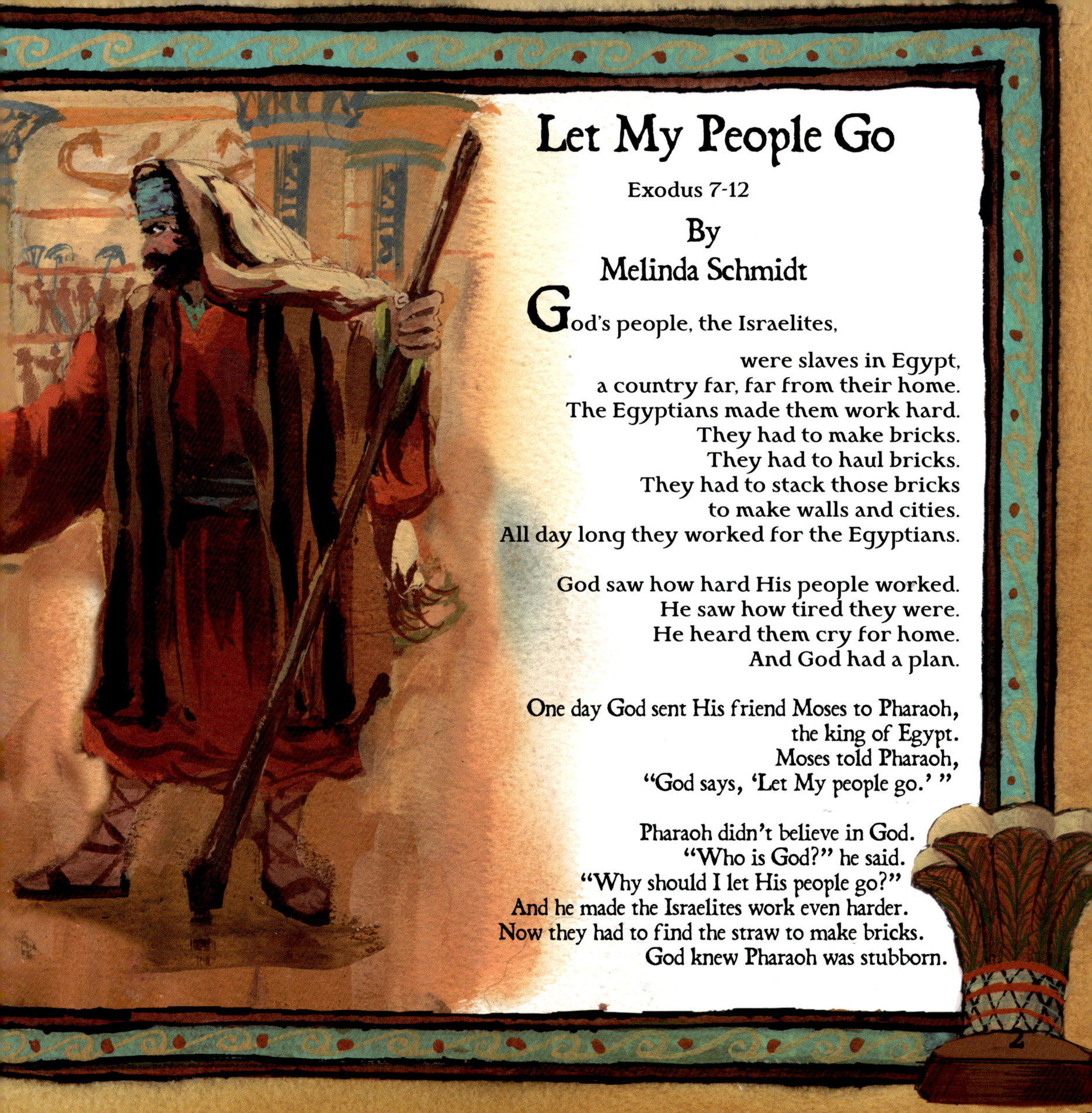

Let My People Go

Exodus 7-12

By
Melinda Schmidt

God's people, the Israelites,

were slaves in Egypt,
a country far, far from their home.
The Egyptians made them work hard.
They had to make bricks.
They had to haul bricks.
They had to stack those bricks
to make walls and cities.
All day long they worked for the Egyptians.

God saw how hard His people worked.
He saw how tired they were.
He heard them cry for home.
And God had a plan.

One day God sent His friend Moses to Pharaoh,
the king of Egypt.
Moses told Pharaoh,
"God says, 'Let My people go.'"

Pharaoh didn't believe in God.
"Who is God?" he said.
"Why should I let His people go?"
And he made the Israelites work even harder.
Now they had to find the straw to make bricks.
God knew Pharaoh was stubborn.

He knew Pharaoh would say No!
But God was going to free His people.
Everyone who heard about it would know that God is God.

God sent Moses to Pharaoh again.
"God says, 'Let My people go,'" Moses told Pharaoh.

"No!" said Pharaoh.

Moses stretched his staff over the Nile River
and it turned to blood, red and thick.
Fish choked and died.
The blood stayed for seven days.
It smelled bad.

Again Moses said to Pharaoh,
"God says, 'Let My people go.'"

"No!" said Pharaoh.

Moses pointed his staff to the north.
He pointed it east and west and south.
Tiny green frogs hopped out of the Nile River.
They hopped out of marshes.
They hopped out of canals.
Tiny green frogs hopped into houses
and into beds and into bread.
Then they died.
The Egyptians gathered them in baskets
and piled them in the fields.

They turned black and stinky.

Still Pharaoh said, "NO!"

Next, God turned the dust to lice—
lice everywhere. People scratched and swatted.
Animals bawled and rubbed
against houses and trees.

"No!" said Pharaoh.

Then came millions of flies. They buzzed.
They bit. Flies were everywhere.

"No!" said Pharaoh.

The animals got sick. Horses and donkeys
died. Sheep and cattle and camels died.

And Pharaoh still said, "No!"

People got boils, hard, swollen sores
that hurt so badly they couldn't walk.

"No!" Pharaoh said.
"You cannot go!"

Moses stretched his hand to the sky.
Black clouds blew in. Lightning flashed.
It ran along the ground in sizzling balls of fire.
Thunder crashed. Hail pounded down.
It flattened the crops.
It broke the trees.
It killed the animals left outside.

"No!" Pharaoh said. "You cannot go!"

Moses raised his rod, and an east wind began to blow. It blew all day and it blew all night. The next morning locusts came, rolling black clouds of locusts. Hungry locusts covered the ground. They munched, munched, munched everything left by the hail—crushed fruit hanging on trees, the stubble of the barley, broken reeds in the Nile.

"No!" said Pharaoh.

Moses stretched his hand high toward the sky. It got very, very dark in the middle of the day. For three days there was no moon, no stars, no ray of light. Pharaoh couldn't see his hand in front of his face. People couldn't leave their houses. There was nothing to see, nothing to do, nowhere to go in that dark land.

Pharaoh said, "No!"

One more time Moses went to Pharaoh. "God says, 'Let My people go.'"

Pharaoh was angry. "No!" he shouted. "Get out of my sight! Do not come back!"

"Very well!" Moses thumped his staff on the floor.
"You will never see me again.
God will bring one more great trouble,
and then you will let us go."
Moses turned his back on Pharaoh and walked out.

At midnight Death struck in the homes
of all who didn't believe God.
In every home the oldest child died.
The baker's oldest child died.
The basket weaver's oldest child died.
The oldest child of the poorest maid died.
Even the cow's first calf died.

And Pharaoh's oldest son died.

In hut and palace people cried.
Pharaoh cried.
How Pharaoh wished he had obeyed God!
Now he knew that God is God.

He sent a messenger to Moses.
"Go!" he said. "Get out of Egypt!"

The Israelites were ready to go.
That very night they marched out of Egypt.
Fathers and mothers shouted for joy.
Girls sang as they carried little brothers and sisters.
Boys ran and wrestled
as they drove the sheep and cattle.

No more bricks to make for Pharaoh.
No more walls and cities to build for Pharaoh.
No more hard, hard work for Pharaoh.

Free! God had set them free!

The Widow's Oil

II Kings 4:1-7
By
Jillian Boese

Two boys hid behind a bush.
A man was pounding at their door.
They wondered who he was.
He wasn't their uncle.
Their uncle was much shorter.
He wasn't their grandfather.
Their grandfather was much older.
He certainly wasn't their father.
Their father wouldn't knock, and besides,
their father was dead.

The door swung open. The man went inside.
He talked to their mother in a loud angry voice.
Then he stalked away down the dusty road.

Their mother came out of the house.
She was crying.
She told the boys to wait at home.
Then down the road she hurried
toward the prophet Elisha's house.

The prophet met her at the door.
She fell down at his feet and cried,
"Master, my husband is dead.
You know that he feared the Lord.
Now the creditor has come
and my two sons must go to be his slaves.

Elisha frowned and scratched his
woolly cheek.
"What shall I do for you?" he asked.
"What do you have in your house?"

She thought about the single
chair, the little sack of meal,
the scraps of wool.

She said, "I really don't
have anything
except a pot of oil."

Then Elisha said, "Go.
Borrow vessels from your neighbors—
vessels old and new, even empty vessels.
Borrow not a few.
Bring them inside your house
and shut the door. Then take your
pot of oil
and pour it into all those vessels."

The widow ran back home.
She hoped the man had not come back.
She hoped her boys would still be there.
Ah, there they were,
playing with a toad beside the path.

She called to them and sent them out,
up one street and down another,
calling, knocking, begging at each door.
"Have you any empty vessels?
We will bring them back.
We only need them for today."

They borrowed
 many vessels.
 Big vessels,
 small vessels,
 short vessels,
 tall vessels,
 narrow vessels,
 wide vessels,
 matching side-by-side
 vessels.

Their mother stood and counted
as they brought them into the house.
Finally, she said, "Enough."

They shut the door.
The widow took her pot of oil.
She held it to the light
and looked inside.
She shook her head.

"What, Mother, what?"
the two boys cried.

"Elisha said to fill these jars,"
she answered.

Their eyes grew wide.
"Fill all these jars
with one small pot?
How ever can that be?"

The widow poured some oil
into a tiny vessel.
She filled it up.
She poured some oil
into a bigger vessel.
She filled it up.
She poured some oil
into a big, fat vessel.
She filled it up.

The boys stood still.
Nobody said a word.
One by one she chose a vessel.
One by one she filled them.
One by one they lined them up,
trying not to spill them.

"Bring me yet another vessel,"
said the widow.

"There is not a vessel more,"
the boys replied.

The widow looked inside her
little pot.
"The oil is gone," she said.
"All gone."
Now we must go
and sell the oil."

So one by one they took the jars
from door to door.
Their friends were pleased
to get their vessels back.
They gladly paid fair price for all the oil.

If they had known that this was special oil,
they might have wanted more. This oil was like a gift of gold.
A gift of gold from God.

They sold it all. There was enough—enough to pay the creditor,
enough to buy more food. The widow's heart was full.
She smiled at her boys.
"God gave enough," she said.
"Enough to fill the vessels. Enough to fill our hearts."

God always gives enough.

GOD CARES FOR HIS FRIENDS

II Kings 6
By
Betsy Unruh

"Who is telling their king my plans?"

God and Elisha were old, old friends.
When God called Elisha to be a prophet,
Elisha left his oxen
and followed God.
When Elisha needed to cross the river,
God parted the water
so Elisha could walk on dry ground.
When naughty children made fun of Elisha,
God sent angry mama bears
to teach those children not to tease His friend.
Elisha knew God would always help him.
God knew Elisha would always obey Him.

The wicked enemy king of Syria
wanted to fight God's people.
He made plan after plan.
Each plan was sure to work,
but each plan failed.
Every time he went out to fight,
God's people knew what he was planning
and were ready for him.
Every time they fought, God's people won.

"Who is telling the king of Israel my plans?" the king of Syria asked his men. "I can whisper a plan in my bedroom, and God's people know about it before morning. One of you is a spy!"

"None of us are spies, O king," answered his men. "It is Elisha, God's friend, who knows everything we plan. He tells their king what we are thinking. He is a wise man, a strong enemy."

"Then we must capture this wise man, this strong enemy!" the king of Syria demanded. "As long as he is living, we will never win a battle! Where does he stay?"

Secret spies went out to find God's friend. They came back in a hurry. "We have found him in Dothan," they told the king.

"Then go straightway to Dothan," the king ordered, "with horses and chariots and a great host of men! Capture Elisha and bring him back to me."

Quickly, quickly, the enemy soldiers gathered their spears and swords. Quickly, quickly, they jumped into their chariots and rode to Dothan. Quickly, quietly, in the darkness, they surrounded the whole city. Elisha, God's friend, was caught in a trap.

Early in the morning, when the sun was just climbing over the dusty mountains, Elisha's servant woke, and stretched, and stepped outside. He looked out over the hills and saw— an army of soldiers! Soldiers, soldiers, everywhere he looked— to the north, to the south, to the east, to the west. Soldiers! Enemies!

He ran back to Elisha, panting and afraid. "Master!" He fell on his knees before Elisha. "The army of Syria surrounds us! We must hide! Where can we go? What shall we do?"

Elisha, God's friend, looked up. His eyes were calm. He folded his hands on the scroll he was reading and smiled at his servant.
"Don't be afraid," he said. "We have an army, too—the army of God."

"But master! We will be captured or—or even killed!"
The servant's voice shook. He jumped to his feet.
"We must run!"

Quietly Elisha bowed his old head and prayed, not for himself, but for his servant.
"Lord, open the eyes of this young man, so he can see what I see, so he can know how great You are."

Then God, Elisha's friend, did what Elisha asked.
He opened the servant's eyes,
and the servant looked out to the dusty mountains.

There, in the light of the early morning sun,
he saw another army—
horses and chariots made of fire,
manes streaming gold, wheels flashing brighter than the sun.
God's fiery horses galloped between Elisha and the army of Syria,
and no enemies could get through to harm them.
Together, Elisha and his servant watched the flaming horses sweep across the mountains.

Then Elisha and his servant—and God—went down to meet the enemy army. The enemies couldn't hurt them. They couldn't even see them, because God, Elisha's mighty Friend, made every soldier in the army blind.
"Come," Elisha told the soldiers.
"I will take you where you need to go."

The soldiers followed Elisha right into Samaria where the king of Israel waited for them. Then God opened their eyes so they could see. They saw Elisha, the man they wanted to capture. They saw they were surrounded by God's people. They saw they were the captives now.

Elisha's king was thrilled to see so many enemies in his power.
"My father," he asked, "shall I smite them? Shall I smite them?"

"No," Elisha told him. "Feed them, and send them back to their own king and their own land. They won't come back anymore."
The king gave every enemy soldier a loaf of bread. He gave every soldier a drink of cool water. Then he sent them away, and they never came back to fight God's people again.

God's people were safe.
Elisha was safe.
God cares for His friends, and God and Elisha were old, old friends.

Jeremiah Speaks God's Word

The book of Jeremiah
By
Vila Gingerich

People in Jerusalem were tired of God's prophet.
Year after year he told them they were wrong.
Year after year he shouted warnings.

"You disobey God," he cried in the market.
"You worship idols. God is not pleased."

The people didn't want to get rid of their idols.
When Jeremiah preached, they rolled their eyes.
They whispered behind their hands.
They hid in nearby shops.

But Jeremiah's words found them.
"God is kind. If you repent, He will not be angry with you."

The people laughed.
"There goes that prophet," they said.
"He is always full of bad news."

All across the city, Jeremiah's words rang.
"The harvest is past. The summer is over.
And we are not saved."

But nobody listened.

Long ago,
When God called him to be a prophet,
Jeremiah had argued.
"But—but I am just a boy," he had said.

"Don't be afraid," God had told him.
"I have put my words in your mouth.
I am with you."

Now, Jeremiah slumped against a stone wall.
He ran his hands through his sweaty hair.
"Oh Lord," he said.
"Everyone makes fun of me. Even my family.
I get so tired of it." He sighed.
"I thought I might stop preaching," he said.
"But, oh Lord, Your words burn like fire in my heart.
I can't stop speaking about You."

Jeremiah trudged back through
the wicked city. He straightened his shoulders
and lifted his head. As long as God gave him
words, he would speak.

Years passed, Jeremiah preached,
and still people sinned.

Four princes grew angry with Jeremiah.
"This prophet speaks only gloomy words,"
one said. "He makes people sad and afraid.
He always wishes bad things on us."

One day the princes called their soldiers.
The soldiers captured Jeremiah
and dragged him across the courtyard.
They uncovered a hole, a hole too wide
to step across. Musty air wafted up
from the empty blackness.

The men tied a rope around Jeremiah
and heaved him over the edge.
They didn't slow down
when he bumped the sharp edge.
They didn't stop when he groaned.
Roughly they lowered him
into the hole and covered it.

Down, deeper, darker.
Jeremiah couldn't see a thing,
not even his own hands.

His toes felt mud, clammy and slick.
Jeremiah jerked up his knees, but he
landed deep in the sticky muck.
He threw out his hands, and slime
splashed all the way to his elbows.

Carefully his fingers reached
into the darkness.
Only mud, mud, and more mud.
It sucked at his feet when he
tried to walk. It covered his face
when he tried to sleep.

For hours, days, Jeremiah waited.
Hour after hour he prayed.
He wondered if God still heard.

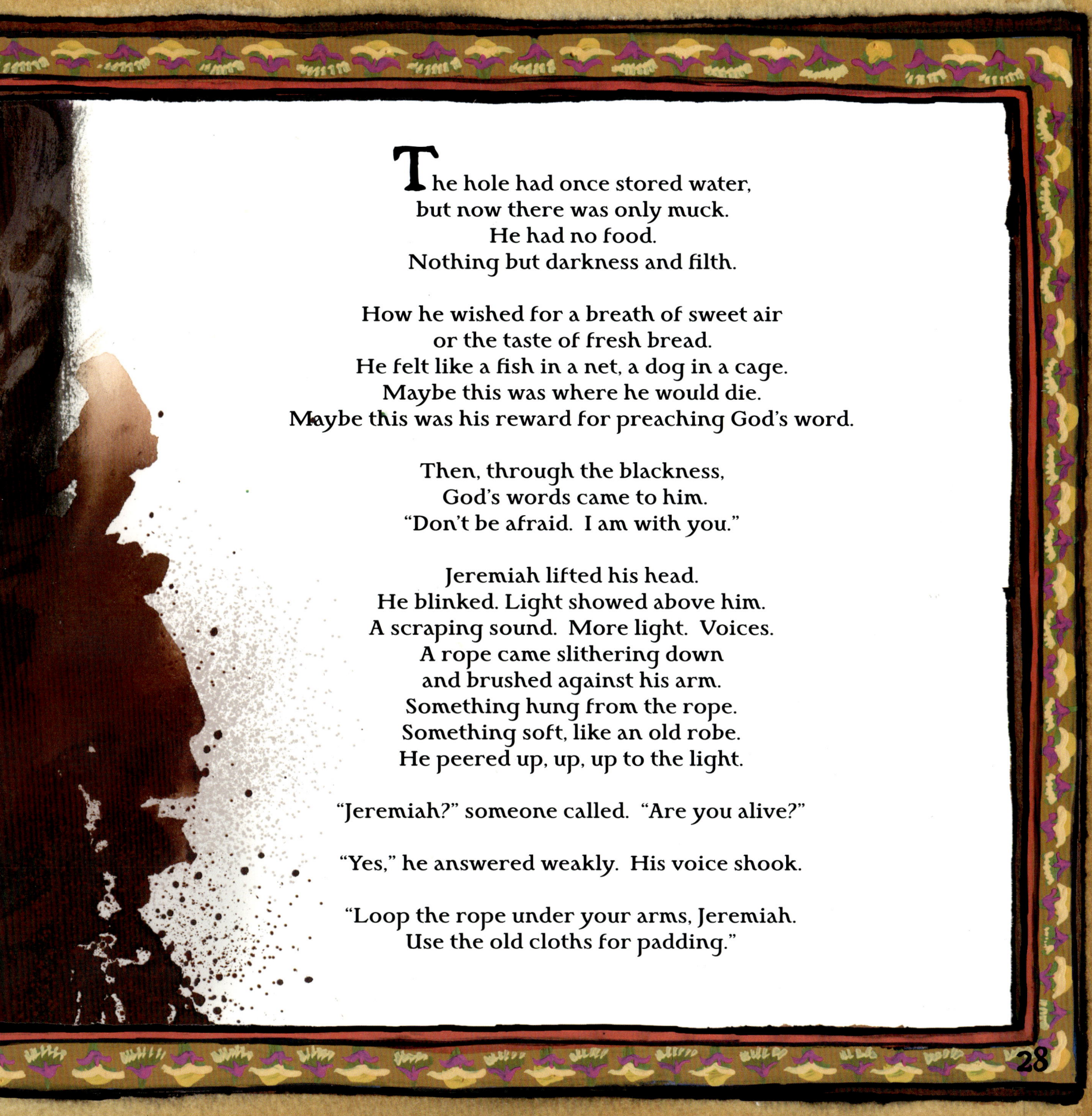

The hole had once stored water,
but now there was only muck.
He had no food.
Nothing but darkness and filth.

How he wished for a breath of sweet air
or the taste of fresh bread.
He felt like a fish in a net, a dog in a cage.
Maybe this was where he would die.
Maybe this was his reward for preaching God's word.

Then, through the blackness,
God's words came to him.
"Don't be afraid. I am with you."

Jeremiah lifted his head.
He blinked. Light showed above him.
A scraping sound. More light. Voices.
A rope came slithering down
and brushed against his arm.
Something hung from the rope.
Something soft, like an old robe.
He peered up, up, up to the light.

"Jeremiah?" someone called. "Are you alive?"

"Yes," he answered weakly. His voice shook.

"Loop the rope under your arms, Jeremiah.
Use the old cloths for padding."

Heart racing joyously,
Jeremiah tucked the rags under his arms.
He made the rope tight with trembling fingers.

"Ready!" he called.

Above him someone began drawing up the rope.
The mud clutched at him. The rope tightened. His bones ached.
A hard jerk, and some of the mud fell away.
A wrench, a tug, and he was free!
A long, smooth pull and Jeremiah stood tottering
on dry, sweet ground.
Squinting against the light,
he could see his smiling friend, a servant of the king.

"Friend," the man spoke, grasping Jeremiah's filthy arm.
"I went to the king. I told him you would die in the mud.
I begged for your life."

Jeremiah's eyes burned in the bright sunlight.
Tears trickled down his face.
He wrapped an arm around his faithful friend.

The air was warm. A breeze blew. Birds sang.
God had not forgotten him in the pit. God was with him still.
He lifted his hands in thanksgiving.
Perhaps God's people still would not listen.
But God's word was in his heart,
and he would speak it over and over again.

Jeremiah's friend, a servant of the king.

Nebuchadnezzar

Daniel 4

By
Betsy Unruh

Nebuchadnezzar, that great king,
that proud and powerful ruler of
mighty Babylon, slept soundly in his golden bed.
His battles were fought.
His enemies were conquered.
He was the greatest king in all the world.

But one night Nebuchadnezzar dreamed
a dream, a bad dream, and
that morning he woke up shivering
between his silken sheets.

He scowled as he sat up in bed.
"Call my magicians," he ordered his servants.
 "Call my astrologers, and call my wise men to me."
He knew they would come.
They must come. They had to come,
or go, or do anything he said,
because he was king.

Magicians, astrologers, and wise men filed in,
fine robes rippling uneasily
as they bowed low.
"O mighty king, live forever.
 Tell us, what troubles you?"

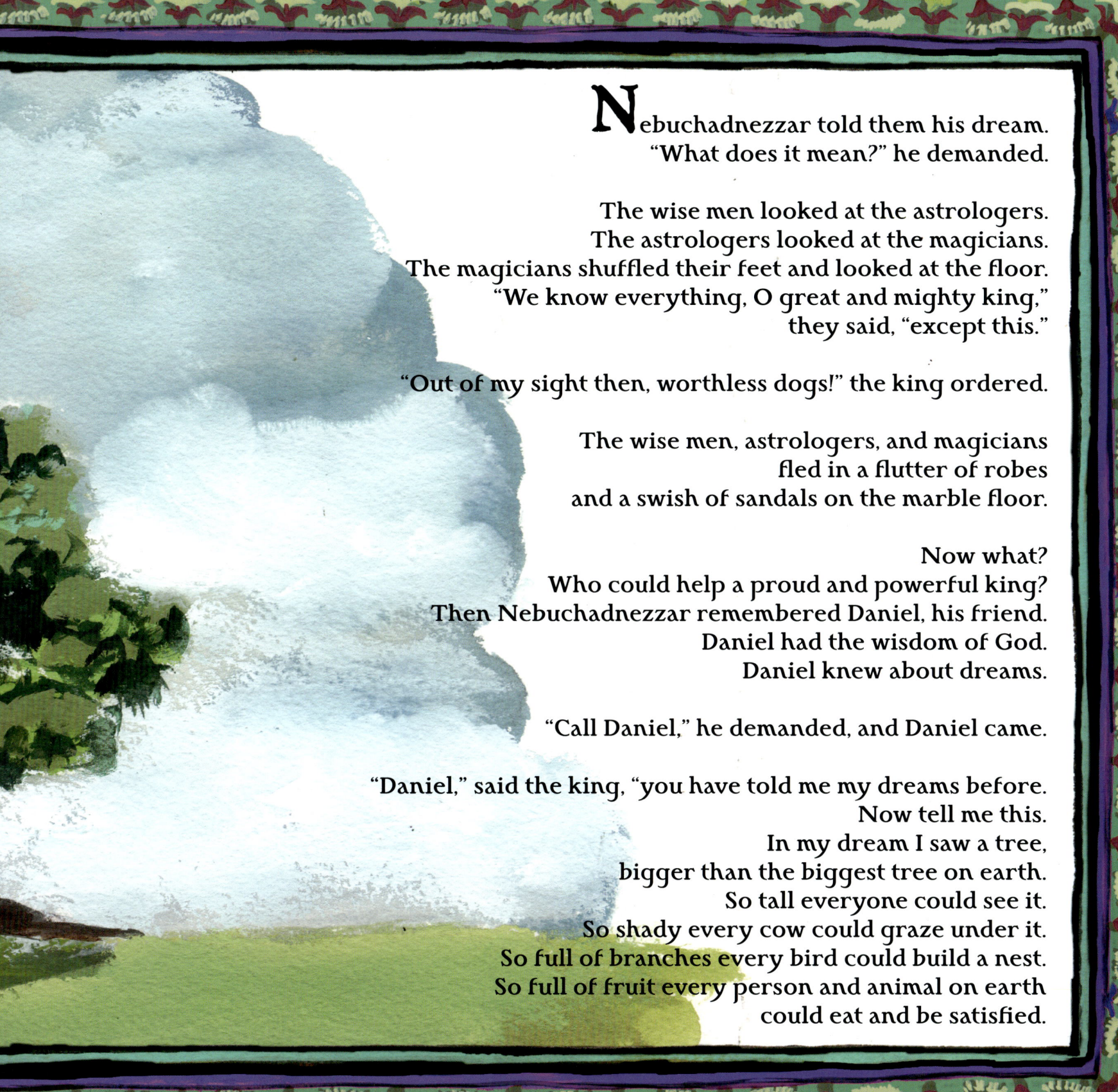

Nebuchadnezzar told them his dream.
"What does it mean?" he demanded.

The wise men looked at the astrologers.
The astrologers looked at the magicians.
The magicians shuffled their feet and looked at the floor.
"We know everything, O great and mighty king,"
they said, "except this."

"Out of my sight then, worthless dogs!" the king ordered.

The wise men, astrologers, and magicians
fled in a flutter of robes
and a swish of sandals on the marble floor.

Now what?
Who could help a proud and powerful king?
Then Nebuchadnezzar remembered Daniel, his friend.
Daniel had the wisdom of God.
Daniel knew about dreams.

"Call Daniel," he demanded, and Daniel came.

"Daniel," said the king, "you have told me my dreams before.
Now tell me this.
In my dream I saw a tree,
bigger than the biggest tree on earth.
So tall everyone could see it.
So shady every cow could graze under it.
So full of branches every bird could build a nest.
So full of fruit every person and animal on earth
could eat and be satisfied.

"Then I saw
an angel come from heaven.
'Cut down the tree!' the angel cried.
'Cut off its branches,
shake off its leaves,
scatter its fruit.
But leave the stump rooted in the ground
among the tender grasses of the field.
Let dew from heaven fall on it.
Let animals graze around it
seven years
until everyone on earth will know
God rules over all.'

"All my wise men could not tell me
what my dream means, Daniel,
but I know you can."

Daniel shut his eyes.
God had told him what the dream meant,
but he did not speak for
one long hour.

Finally, the king said,
"Tell me, Daniel. Don't be afraid."

Then Daniel spoke.
"O king, I wish this dream was happening
to your worst enemies.
The strong, mighty tree is you.

You are the greatest king on earth,
and your kingdom reaches over all the land and sea.
But there is a God greater than you.

"He gave you your kingdom, and He will take it away
unless you learn to worship Him.
You will be driven out of your palace.
You will live with wild animals
for seven years until you know that God rules over all.
Listen, O king, and turn away from your pride."

But the king did not listen. A whole year went by,
and he was still the proud and powerful king of Babylon.
One day he looked around his lovely palace and said,
"I have built all this by my mighty power, for my own majesty.
This is mine, all mine, made by me."

Even as he spoke those proud words, a voice fell from Heaven.
"O King Nebuchadnezzar," God's voice told him, "you have lost your kingdom."
Before an hour had passed, King Nebuchadnezzar lost everything,
even his mind.

His servants took sticks
and drove him out of his palace
into the fields.
He ate grass like a cow.
His hair fell in dirty strings over
his face. His fingernails and
toenails curled like birds' claws.
He slept on hard dirt,
instead of on a soft bed. He woke
in the mornings shivering
and dripping with dew.
Seven long years
he lived alone in the
pasture, wild as any animal.

One day Nebuchadnezzar, that poor, crazy, old man,
looked up from the grass he was chewing.
He looked up, up, up. He saw the sun.
He saw the clouds. He saw God's beautiful sky.
Just like that, his mind came back to him, and he praised God.

"O Lord, You are God, and You live forever.
You gave me my kingdom, and You took it away.
You can do anything, and no one can stop You.
You rule over all."

Nebuchadnezzar returned to his palace,
his mighty kingdom, and his golden bed.
He sang as he took a bath.
He prayed as the barber cut his hair.
Once again, he became the powerful king of Babylon.

But with one big difference.
He had left his ugly pride
behind him in that field.
"Praise God with me!"
he told his friends.
"Let us serve God,
Daniel's God,
the mighty God
who will
forever
rule over all!"

Belshazzar
Daniel 5

By

Betsy Unruh

Night was falling fast in Babylon.
Palm trees faded into feathery shadows.
Fountains splashed silver in the moonlight.
It was going-home time, supper-time, bed-time
in Babylon.
But outside the strong walls of Babylon,
an enemy army camped.
On the far side of the river, enemy soldiers
waited for darkness to fall.

Belshazzar, proud and powerful king
of mighty Babylon, was not ready for sleep.
"Prepare a feast!" he commanded.
"Our city walls are thick and strong.
We have food enough for twenty years
of fighting the enemy. We will show
those soldiers we aren't afraid!"

In every corner of Babylon, lords and
ladies put on their finest robes
and shiniest jewels.
From every corner of Babylon,
a thousand lords and ladies started
toward Belshazzar's feast.
They passed the tall towers
Belshazzar had built for his gods.

They passed the huge stone lion Belshazzar had built to worship.
They passed the river where water lapped at the shore in the moonlight,
enemy soldiers hiding on the other side.

Candlelight gleamed on the walls at Belshazzar's feast.
Laughter and music echoed from every corner.
Purple wine flowed into golden goblets.

"More wine!" Belshazzar bellowed.
 "And bring the gold and silver vessels
that my father brought
from the temple in Jerusalem.
We will drink from them tonight!"

Belshazzar's servants shivered.
The vessels from the temple?
They didn't belong to Belshazzar
 or even to his gods of gold and silver.
They belonged to a mighty God.
No one, not even a powerful king of Babylon,
should drink from those vessels.

But Belshazzar was king, so they brought the vessels and filled them up with wine.
Now the feast was even better. Lords told stories. Ladies giggled.
No one thought about the enemy soldiers waiting in the darkness.
No one thought about the true God whose vessels they were using.

In the middle of the feast, Belshazzar looked up.
He stared, his eyes growing wide.
Up there, above the candlelight,
something was moving.
A hand glowed in the darkness,
tracing words with a finger on the stone.

MENE MENE—the hand wrote.
Belshazzar's face paled. Whose hand was it?
What did those strange words mean?
TEKEL—The finger left a fiery trail of words behind it.
The golden goblet dropped
from Belshazzar's hand.
Wine dripped
into a purple puddle
on the floor.
UPHARSIN—wrote the hand.
And disappeared.
The words remained,
glowing on the wall.

Belshazzar's robe quivered. His knees shook as he tried to stand.
"C—c—call my magicians!" His voice shook.
"Call my astrologers! Call my wise men to me!
I will give them a—a golden chain, a scarlet robe, and—and a place in my kingdom if they tell me what this means!" Servants hurried out.

Wise men hurried in. They stared at the wall. Never had they seen words like these. Not for a robe or a chain or a throne could they say what the words meant. Shaking their heads and mumbling excuses, they slunk away.

The feast was forgotten. Everyone stared at the wall.
Then the queen walked quietly up to Belshazzar.
"My lord," she said, "there is a man who can help. Daniel had wisdom and light for your father Nebuchadnezzar,
and he will have wisdom for you."

"Call Daniel!" the king ordered, and Daniel came.

"I have heard of you, Daniel, and your wisdom," said the king.
"A scarlet robe, a golden chain, and a place in my kingdom are yours if you tell me what these words say."

"You may keep your robe, your chain, and a place in your kingdom, O king," Daniel answered.
"I have no need of them.

"Your father Nebuchadnezzar was a mighty king,
but God humbled him.
You are even prouder than your father, and God will humble you too."

Belshazzar scowled.

Daniel went on. "You drink wine from vessels out of God's temple,
but you do not worship Him.
Instead you serve gods made from silver and gold, brass and iron,
wood and stone. It was God's hand who
wrote on the wall, and this is what He has to say to you.

"MENE—God has numbered your kingdom and has finished it.
TEKEL—You are weighed in God's balance and found wanting.
UPHARSIN—Your kingdom is divided and given to your enemies."

Belshazzar gave Daniel the scarlet robe and the golden chain
and promised him a place in the kingdom. Then he sent Daniel away.

But Belshazzar did not fall on his knees.
He did not pray to the Almighty God.
God had given him one last chance, but Belshazzar didn't take it.
While Belshazzar and his lords drank wine from
God's golden vessels, the enemy soldiers built a dam across
Babylon's mighty river.
Quietly, quietly, in the darkness, they crossed the dry riverbed
into the city. With a clashing of swords and a crashing
of trumpets they captured the city
and Belshazzar and all his lords and ladies.
Belshazzar was killed. Enemies took his mighty kingdom.

God's words were true, and night fell fast on Babylon.

Jonah
Jonah 1 & 2
By
Dena Unruh

"Go to Nineveh," God told his prophet Jonah.
"Tell the people I will destroy their wicked city in forty days
unless they repent."

"Those people?" Jonah snorted. "Don't save them.
They stole our animals and plundered our cities."
Besides, Nineveh had a strong wall, one hundred feet high,
and wide enough for three chariots.

Jonah didn't go to Nineveh.
He ran away to Joppa,
five hundred and fifty miles from Nineveh.
From there he caught a ship to far-off Tarshish.

Jonah stood on the deck. The wind pushed against him.
It pushed against the sails.
It pushed the boat away from shore.

Jonah let out a long breath. Whew!
Soon he would be far, far away from Nineveh.
He scrambled to the bottom of the boat and lay down on a coil of rope.

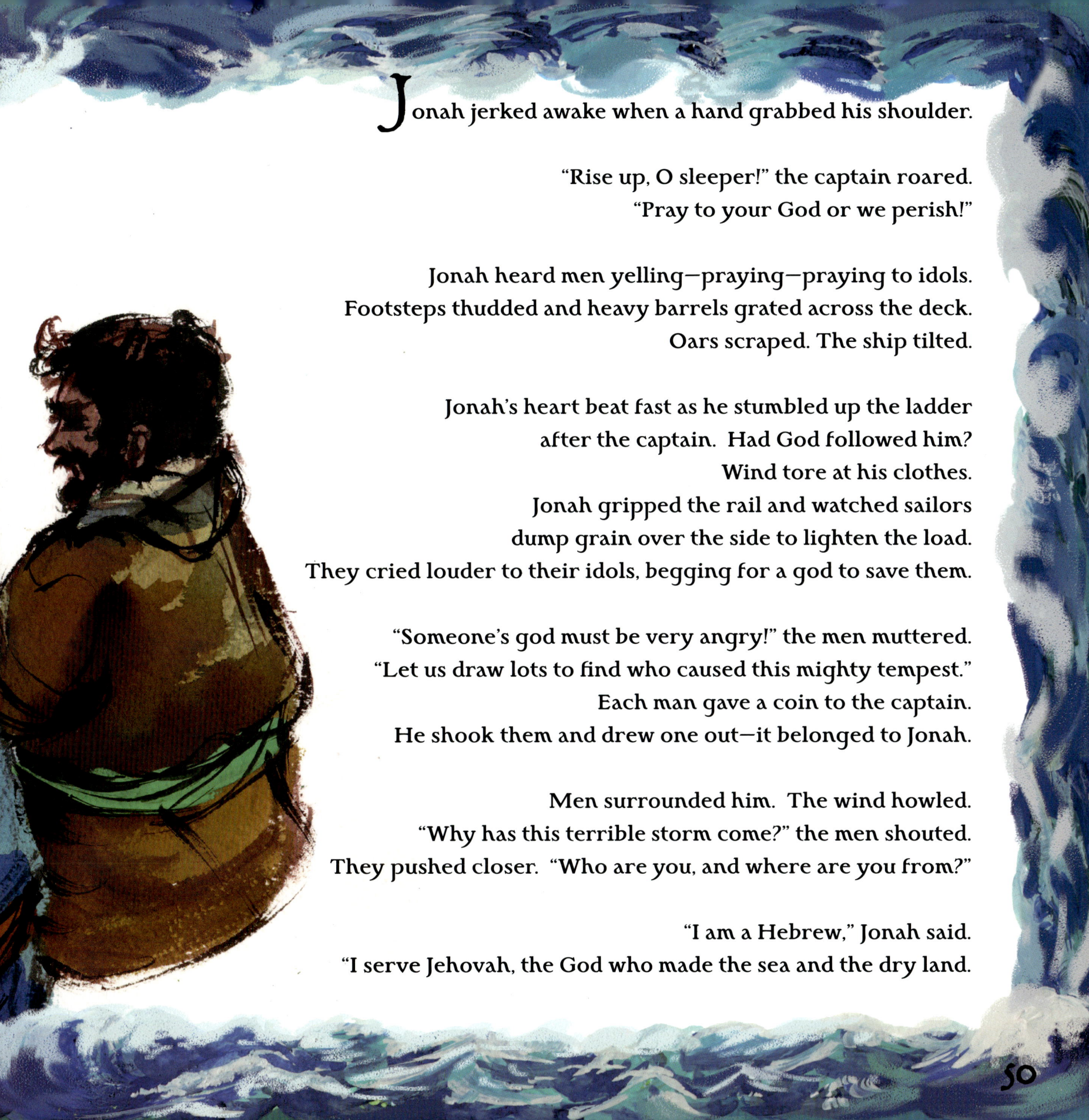

Jonah jerked awake when a hand grabbed his shoulder.

"Rise up, O sleeper!" the captain roared.
"Pray to your God or we perish!"

Jonah heard men yelling—praying—praying to idols.
Footsteps thudded and heavy barrels grated across the deck.
Oars scraped. The ship tilted.

Jonah's heart beat fast as he stumbled up the ladder
after the captain. Had God followed him?
Wind tore at his clothes.
Jonah gripped the rail and watched sailors
dump grain over the side to lighten the load.
They cried louder to their idols, begging for a god to save them.

"Someone's god must be very angry!" the men muttered.
"Let us draw lots to find who caused this mighty tempest."
Each man gave a coin to the captain.
He shook them and drew one out—it belonged to Jonah.

Men surrounded him. The wind howled.
"Why has this terrible storm come?" the men shouted.
They pushed closer. "Who are you, and where are you from?"

"I am a Hebrew," Jonah said.
"I serve Jehovah, the God who made the sea and the dry land.

He sent this storm because I disobeyed."

An old man scowled. His hands shook.
"Why did you do this thing?" he said. "Will we all die?"
The men grabbed for handholds as water soaked them.
Pellets of rain stung their faces.

Jonah cried, "Throw me out into the sea
and the storm will stop."

They pleaded with God, and tears ran with the rain.
"We don't want to die in this storm.
We don't want Jonah to drown."

The storm raged. The ship groaned.
The men rowed, but God had sent the storm,
and the men were not stronger than the storm.

Finally, the men picked up Jonah
by his hands and his feet.
"O Jehovah," the men prayed,
"let us not perish for this man's life."

They swung Jonah—a one, and a two, and a three—
and they flung him overboard.
Splash! Down, down, down.

But Jonah's God was the real God.

The storm stopped.
The wind died.
The waves fell back into the quiet ocean.
From deep in the sea, God sent a fish—
a humongous fish.
The fish saw Jonah and opened its mouth—
its enormous mouth.
With a powerful swish of its tail,
 it spun and opened its great mouth around Jonah.
It gulped.
It swallowed.

"Save me, O God, save me!" Jonah cried.
It was dark.
The smell made him gag. Little fish poked him.
Weeds wrapped around his head.
His hands were slimy.
For three days and three nights, Jonah did not sleep.
His eyes burned.
He was hungry. He hurt all over.
But Jonah did not die. In the belly of the fish,
Jonah prayed.

God heard Jonah.
When Jonah prayed from the bottom of the ocean,
God heard.
From the weeds and slime, when Jonah called, God heard.

God spoke to that fish.

The fish swam to shore.
Up, out of its stomach, came Jonah
and plopped down on the sand.
Jonah raised his head. He was free!

His skin was red and white
and sore and wrinkled.
He smelled like sour fish.
Slime dripped from his hair.
He wobbled when he stood up.
But he was alive! He was free!
Jonah lifted his hands to heaven.
He sang. He prayed.
"Salvation comes from Jehovah," he said.

God still needed someone
to preach at Nineveh.
"Go to Nineveh," God told Jonah.
"Tell the people I will destroy
their wicked city unless they repent."

And this time, when God said go,
Jonah went.

In the Master's Vineyard

Matthew 20
By
Vila Gingerich

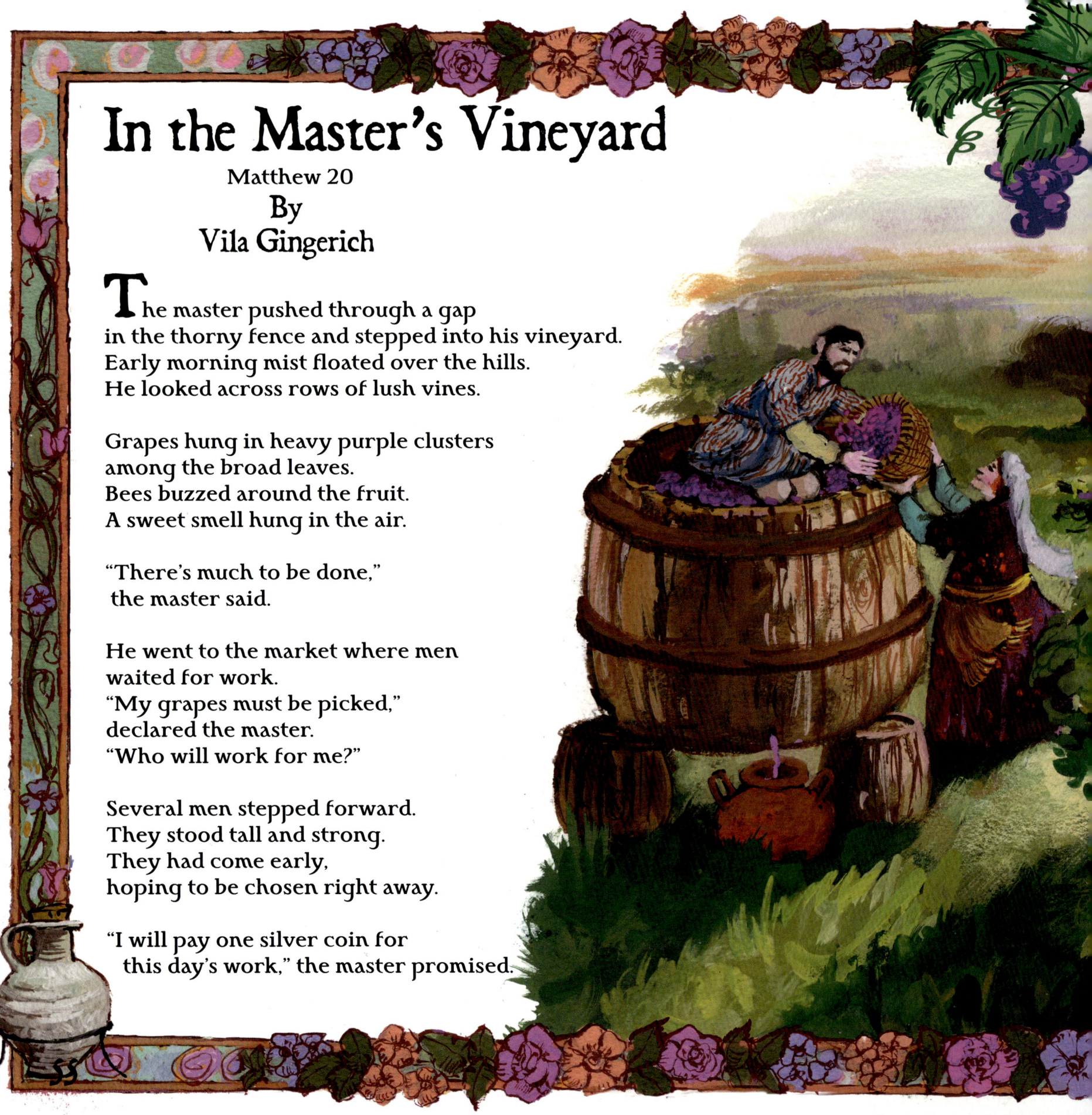

The master pushed through a gap
in the thorny fence and stepped into his vineyard.
Early morning mist floated over the hills.
He looked across rows of lush vines.

Grapes hung in heavy purple clusters
among the broad leaves.
Bees buzzed around the fruit.
A sweet smell hung in the air.

"There's much to be done,"
 the master said.

He went to the market where men
waited for work.
"My grapes must be picked,"
declared the master.
"Who will work for me?"

Several men stepped forward.
They stood tall and strong.
They had come early,
hoping to be chosen right away.

"I will pay one silver coin for
 this day's work," the master promised.

The men agreed and followed the master.
Back to his vineyard they went,
through the gap in the thorny fence,
past the watchman's tower.
They picked up the round woven baskets and began to pick grapes.

At the third hour, when the dew had dried on the vines,
the master looked over his fields.
The vineyard was large. The workers were few.
They picked quickly, but there was much to be done.

The master hurried back into town.
Near a leather shop,
people leaned against a building,
watching the shopkeepers.
One slapped at a fly.
Another yawned.

"Oh, won't you come work in my vineyard?"
the master asked.
"Come now and I'll pay a fair wage."

The men straightened.
They brushed off their hands.
They followed the master to his vineyard
and began to work.

Now the sun beat down on the workers' backs.
Their baskets overflowed with plump grapes.
On and on they worked,
but no one had begun on the hillsides
beyond the watchtower.

At the sixth hour the master left again.
He came back with more workers.

At the ninth hour
he went after still more.

Sometimes the workers begged to rest.
Sometimes they said the sun was too hot.
But the work was not so very hard,
and the master was kind.
Their wages would buy food for their families.

Now, when the master looked over his field,
he saw many bent backs.
He saw many full baskets.
But there was much left to do,
and the grapes in the far corner
might never be picked.

One last time the master went into town.
It was the eleventh hour.
The sun hung low in the western sky.
Several villagers lounged under a tree.
Some of them chatted.
Others slept.

"Come, come," the master said.
"Why are you sitting here all day,
doing nothing?"

"Because nobody hires us."
they answered.

"Hurry down to my vineyard," the master begged,
"Help us work.
I will pay you fairly, one silver coin each."

Now there were workers in every row.
Now the baskets filled more quickly.
Now the master smiled down on his vineyard.

As the sun began to set, the master looked around.
The grapes were picked.
   The fields were clean and empty.
      The harvest was over.

He called his steward.
"Bring in the workers," he said.
"Pay them their wages."

The workers stretched their backs.
They wiped their sweaty foreheads.
They lined up before the steward.

He opened his moneybag and began to sort out coins
while the master watched.

Silver coins glinted in the sun.
Silver coins tumbled from the steward's fingers
 into their waiting hands.

One coin to each worker
who came at the eleventh hour.
One coin to each worker
who came at the ninth hour.
And the sixth hour.
And the third hour.

The workers who had come first waited quietly.
They watched the steward.
They watched those coins.
They had come early.
They had worked all day.
If the people who came in the afternoon each got a silver coin,
how much would they get?

At last the steward came to the first men,
the men who had worked all day.
He handed them each a silver coin.

"What?"
The youngest workman raised his brows
and threw out his hands.
"Is this fair?"

"Master," another workman complained.
"Those men worked only one hour.
You gave them exactly what you gave us,
but we worked all day."

"Even through the hottest part," the youngest man added.

The master put his hand on the young worker's shoulder.
"Friends," he spoke kindly, "I have not wronged you.
Didn't you agree to work for one coin?"

The men nodded.

Well," said the master, "you worked hard,
and I've paid you what I promised, haven't I?"

Yes," the men agreed.

"Friends, take your wages and go to your homes," the master said. He smiled at them.

The workmen walked away.
Past the watchman's tower,
through the gap in the thorny fence,
back toward the village.

Each worker had his wages.
Each worker had money
to buy fish and bread.
Each worker would
rest well that night.

Welcome Home

Luke 15

By Betsy Unruh

Once upon a time, in a country far away,
a farmer had two sons.
He loved them both the same,
even though they were very different.

When the father told stories about God,
the older son listened quietly.
The younger son scratched his ears and yawned.

When the boys sat down at the table,
the older son reached for
soft, warm bread.
The younger son sighed and
dreamed of honeyed figs.

When darkness crept around
their house, the older son
snuggled into soft blankets
with a happy sigh.

The younger son looked out the window at the moonlit fields and thought about sailing ships, mountain palaces, and camel trains crossing desert sands.

As the boys grew up, the older son learned to grow the best barley. With his coins he bought young calves and sturdy sheep. The younger son learned to hunt rats and race donkeys.

He wasted his coins betting on the donkeys and buying honeyed figs.

He got grumpier and grumpier.

Finally, the younger son got so tired of plodding oxen and stubborn calves and weedy wheat and the same old bread day after day that he growled at his father.

"Father, when you die, everything you own will belong to farmer boy there and me. I can't stick around here forever like a mooing old ox, going out to pasture every morning and coming in at night! Give me my money. Now."

What should the father do?
If he gave his son money,
he knew it would soon be all gone.
But he was a wise father,
and he loved his unhappy son.
He divided everything he owned
in two parts and gave each boy his share.

The younger son smiled.
He packed his bags and left for a distant country.
He didn't say goodbye.

He traveled fast and far. He wanted to forget his home,
his father, and especially God.
He made himself sick eating honeyed figs.

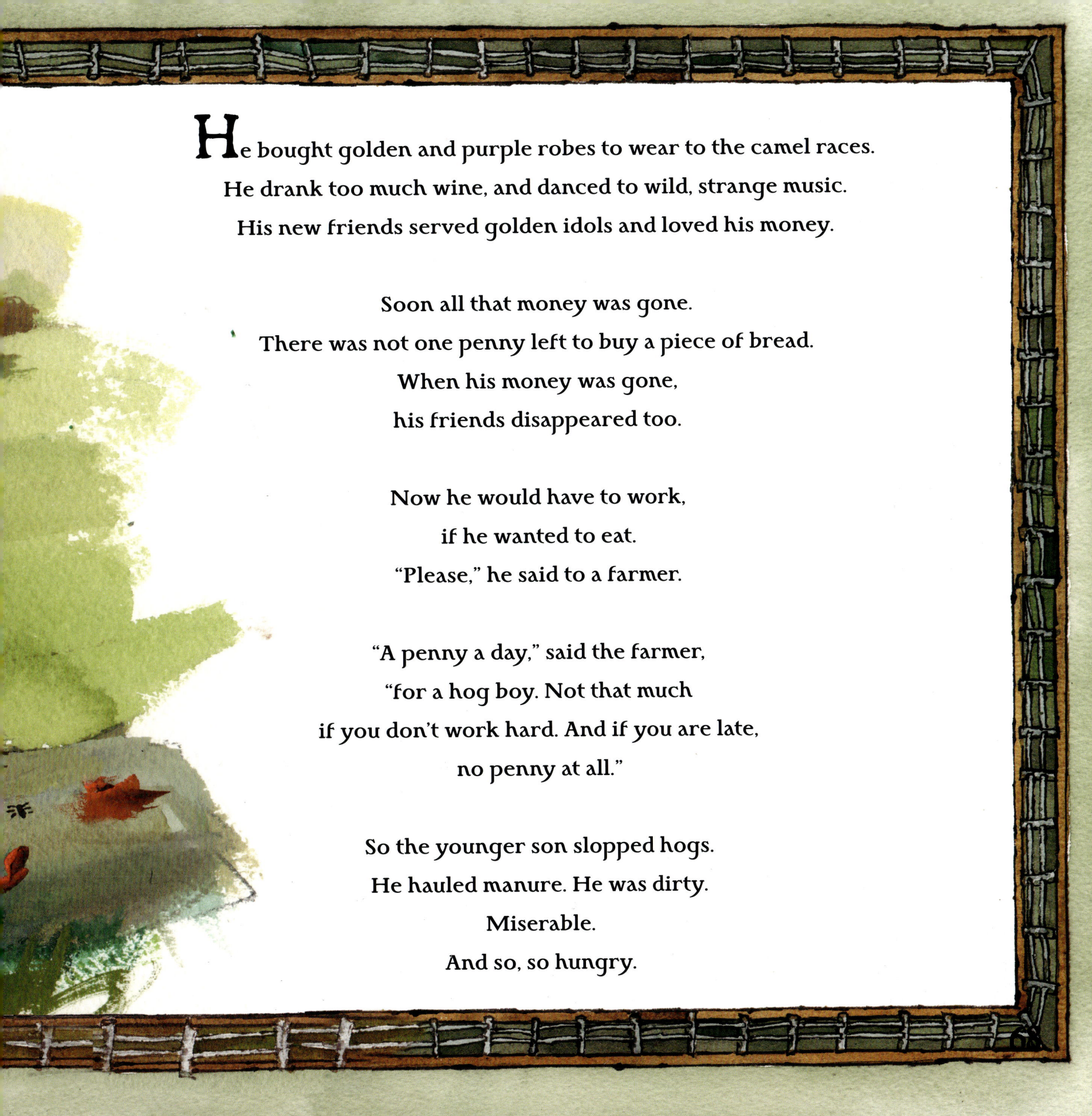

He bought golden and purple robes to wear to the camel races.

He drank too much wine, and danced to wild, strange music.

His new friends served golden idols and loved his money.

Soon all that money was gone.

There was not one penny left to buy a piece of bread.

When his money was gone,

his friends disappeared too.

Now he would have to work,

if he wanted to eat.

"Please," he said to a farmer.

"A penny a day," said the farmer,

"for a hog boy. Not that much

if you don't work hard. And if you are late,

no penny at all."

So the younger son slopped hogs.

He hauled manure. He was dirty.

Miserable.

And so, so hungry.

One day he looked at the empty cornhusks
those greedy hogs were gobbling.
Almost he snatched one for himself.
Then he remembered something.

Back home, he thought, there was always
bread for everyone—
the servants, the ox, even the dogs.
My father was so kind.
But, of course, he has forgotten me by now,
or else he hates me for being so mean.
I could never go back to my father.
I could never look into his face again
after the awful things I said.
I don't deserve to be my father's son,
but I'm so tired of this.
    Maybe—maybe—
        I could feed his ox
            and haul manure for him.
                I am going to ask.

Crawling out of the muddy hog pen,
the younger son started
down the road home.

Back home, the father had not forgotten
his younger son.
Every day he watched the road,
squinting against the sun,
hoping to see his boy.

One day, far down the dusty road,
the father saw someone coming.
His son?

No. It couldn't be his son.
It was a dirty, skinny beggar,
dressed in rags.
No.
Not a beggar.
It was—
Yes!
It was his son!
The father ran, sandals flapping
on the dusty road, to meet his son.

He threw his arms around his boy and cried.

"Father," said the son, looking down at the dusty road,
"I have sinned against God and against you.
I am not worthy to be your son.
Please, let me be your servant."

But the father called to his servants,
"Bring the finest robe for my son. Put my ring
on his hand and new shoes on his feet.
Bring the fattest calf and kill it so we can feast.
I thought my son was dead, but he is alive.
He was lost, but now he is found.
My son is home."

God, our Father, loves us like the father loved his son.
Even when we forget God, He waits and watches and calls us.
When we come to Him like a beggar, with our sins and dirty rags,
He takes us in His arms and says,

"Welcome home."

Thank You, JESUS

Luke 17:11-19

By

Nancy Wiebe

Tobiah had leprosy. Because he had leprosy, he couldn't live at home. He couldn't live in town. He had to live out in the hills in a leper camp where people wouldn't catch his disease.

Every day Tobiah sat by the road watching people, ordinary people, well people, people going to and from their homes. He sat close to the road, but not too close. He didn't want to shout "Unclean! Unclean!" to warn people he was near. Tobiah stretched out his legs in front of him and saw a bruise spreading on his foot, the foot that was already missing a big toe. When had he hurt it? He hadn't noticed a thing. The longer he had leprosy, the less he could feel. The more scaly white patches appeared on his skin. The more scratchy his voice sounded. His eyesight was getting blurry, too. At least he could hear.

Right now he heard huffing and puffing and steps coming up the hill. Michael appeared, red-faced and waving his arms. "Jesus is coming this way!" he shouted, pointing up the road. "My mother sent me a message. He will pass by here today!"

The lepers sat up.

"I will ask Him to heal me," said Reuben. "I have been here the longest. I am the sickest."

"He will heal me." Felix spoke firmly, pressing his stubby fingers together. "I am the son of a rich man."

"I served God when I was well," Asher croaked. "I will be healed."

"Could Jesus heal me?" Tobiah spoke softly.

The lepers laughed. "You are a Samaritan! He won't even look at you."

Tobiah watched the road anyway. The sun rose high. Would Jesus really come? Could Jesus really heal lepers? His head grew heavy and he lay down.

A noise like a swarm of bees woke him up. The buzz turned into voices—high voices, low voices, and loud voices. Tobiah raised his head. The steps of many, many people were stirring up dust into a cloud.

He sat up. Leaning on his walking stick, he pushed and pulled until he was standing. This was his chance. "Jesus, Master, have mercy on me!" he shouted.

Some of the people heard his hoarse voice. They looked at the ten lepers and crowded to the far side of the road.

"Jesus, Master," Tobiah cried again, "have mercy on me!" The other lepers joined him. Tobiah clenched his knobby fists. Tears ran down his face. Jesus must hear him. "Jesus, Master, have mercy on me!" The tramping of feet was almost past.

And then—a Man turned. He came close.

"Jesus," Tobiah whispered.

Jesus looked at each leper on the hillside—at Reuben, at Felix, at Asher, and even at Tobiah. Then He spoke.

"Go show yourselves to the priests," He said.

Tobiah wiped his eyes. Limping, stumbling, the lepers turned and hurried down the road.

"We'll be healed at the temple," Reuben declared. "Then the priests will allow us back into the town."

But this wasn't Tobiah's town. These priests wouldn't want a Samaritan in their temple. Maybe Jesus hadn't meant him. He slowed down. The next hill looked too hard to climb. But Jesus had looked right at him, hadn't He? Jesus had heard him calling.

He took another step. And another. He squinted in the bright sunlight. His throat tickled, and he coughed. He smoothed his wrinkled robe.

He could feel!

Tobiah stared at the other lepers. Their faces glowed. Reuben's skin was pink and smooth. Felix held his hands up high. There were clean scars where the scabs had been. Asher shouted joyously. The lepers that were lepers-no-more reached out to touch each other.

Tobiah spun around. He jumped. He shouted. And he ran all the way back to Jesus.

"Thank you, Jesus!" he cried bowing to the ground. "Thank you! Thank you!" Happy tears ran down his cheeks.

"Weren't there ten men healed?" Jesus asked. "Where are the other nine?" Then He smiled at Tobiah. "Get up," He said. "Go on your way. Your faith has made you whole."

Tobiah got up on one knee. He looked at the smooth skin on his foot, the place where the bruise had been. And then he saw his toes. Four little ones and one big one. He looked at his hands. He looked at his arms. Every scar was gone.

Tobiah stood up. He squared his shoulders. Sunlight warmed his new skin and spread all the way to his happy heart.